# CONTENTS

# WORD HUNT

Look for these words as you read. They will be in **bold**.

**backboard**
(**bak**-bord)

**foul**
(foul)

**jump shot**
(jump shot)

4

SCHOLASTIC
News
Nonfiction Readers®

# Let's Talk Basketball

## by Amanda Miller

Children's Press®
An Imprint of Scholastic Inc.
New York  Toronto  London  Auckland  Sydney
Mexico City  New Delhi  Hong Kong
Danbury, Connecticut

These content vocabulary word builders are for grades 1–2.

Subject Consultant: Thomas Sawyer, EdD, Professor of Recreation and Sport Management, Indiana State University

Reading Consultant: Cecilia Minden-Cupp, PhD, Reading Specialist and Author, Chapel Hill, North Carolina

Photographs © 2009: age fotostock/Dennis MacDonald: 17; Alamy Images: 5 bottom right, 18 (Aflo Photo Agency), 11 (George S. de Blonsky), 4 bottom left, 5 bottom left, 6, 9, 12, 13 (GPI Stock), 4 top, 14 (JupiterImages/Brand X), 20 left (A.T. Willett), 21 right (Laura Wintermantel); Corbis Images: 2, 7 (Rick Burnham/Icon SMI), 23 bottom right (Darryl Dennis/Icon SMI), 19 (Lucy Nicholson/Reuters); Getty Images: cover (Digital Vision), 23 top left (Focus on Sport), 23 top right (Barry Gossage/NBAE), 23 bottom left (Walter Iooss Jr./NBAE), 13 top (Photodisc), 1, 5 top left, 8 left (Mike Powell), 5 top right, 8 right (Michael Turek); PhotoEdit/Michael Newman: back cover, 4 bottom right, 16; Photolibrary/David Madison/Digital Vision: 15; VEER: 20 right (Blend Images Photography), 21 left (Brand X Photography).

Series Design: Simonsays Design!
Book Production: Scholastic Classroom Magazines

Library of Congress Cataloging-in-Publication Data

Miller, Amanda, 1974–
Let's talk basketball / by Amanda Miller.
    p. cm.—(Scholastic news nonfiction readers)
Let's talk basketball
Includes bibliographical references and index.
ISBN-13: 978-0-531-13829-8 (lib. bdg.)  978-0-531-20429-0 (pbk.)
ISBN-10: 0-531-13829-1 (lib. bdg.)  0-531-20429-4 (pbk.)
1. Basketball—Juvenile literature. I. Title. II. Series.
GV885.M54 2009
796.323—dc22                          2008020084

2 3 4 5 6 7 8 9 10 R 18 17 16 15 14 13 12 11 10 09          62

## court
(cort)

## dribbling
(**drib**-ling)

## official
(uh-**fish**-uhl)

## slam dunk
(slam dunk)

# Jump Ball!

It's time to play basketball! A jump ball starts the game. An **official** throws the ball into the air. Then one player from each team tries to tip the ball to her teammates.

official

The jump ball that starts the game is called the opening tip.

A player bounces the ball as he moves on the **court**. That's called **dribbling**. Some players are so good they can dribble the ball between their legs.

**dribbling**

**court**

Players can use only one hand at a time to dribble.

Players pass the ball to their teammates. They want to move the ball closer to the basket so their team can score.

Sometimes, a player from the other team grabs the ball away. That's called a steal.

A player passes the ball in a game of wheelchair basketball.

**Foul**! A foul means someone broke a rule. You are not allowed to kick, push, or hold another player.

If players get too many fouls, they are out of the game.

**foul**

The official blows his whistle when he sees a foul.

A player shoots the ball. He misses! It didn't even get close to the basket. That's an air ball. Sometimes the ball only hits the **backboard** or the rim. That's called a brick.

**backboard**

Air ball! In basketball, many shots do not go in the basket.

Now a player jumps in the air and shoots the ball. This is called a **jump shot**.

The ball goes in the basket. She scores!

**jump
shot**

This player jumps as high as she can to shoot the ball.

Sometimes a player jumps so high he touches the rim. He stuffs the ball into the basket with his hands. That's a **slam dunk**! It's one of the most exciting shots of the game.

**slam dunk**

# THE BASKETBAL

## I point

**Did you know?**
You always have to get the ball into the hoop to score—but not all baskets are worth the same number of points.

## Free Throws
Sometimes, a player gets c "free throw" if the other tea gets a foul. If the ball goes i she scores one point.

# SCOREBOARD

## 2 points

## 3 points

three-point line

### Most Baskets

Most shots in basketball are worth two points.

### Three-Point Shots

If a player shoots a basket from behind the three-point line, he gets three points instead of two.

# YOUR NEW WORDS

**backboard** (**bak**-bord) the board attached to a basketball hoop or net

**court** (cort) an area where basketball is played

**dribbling** (**drib**-ling) bouncing the basketball with one hand, while running

**foul** (foul) an action in sports that is against the rules

**jump shot** (jump shot) when a player tries to score by jumping up and throwing the ball toward the basket

**official** (uh-**fish**-uhl) a person who makes sure the players follow the rules of a game

**slam dunk** (slam dunk) when a player touches the rim of the basket and puts the ball through the hoop with his hands

# FOUR
# BASKETBALL GREATS

ilt Chamberlain

Cynthia Cooper

Michael Jordan

Lisa Leslie

# INDEX

## FIND OUT MORE

**Book:**
Stewart, Wayne. *The Little Giant Book of Basketball Facts.* New York: Sterling Publishing, 2007.

**Website:**
Kids World Sports: Basketball
*http://www.pbskids.org/kws/sports/basketball.html*

## MEET THE AUTHOR

Amanda Miller is a writer and editor for Scholastic. She and her dog, Henry, live in Brooklyn, New York, but they root for the North Carolina Tarheels.